WICCA STARTER KIT

A Beginners' Guide to Wicca Beliefs, Rituals, Magic and Witchcraft

Rose Cunningham

© **Copyright 2019 - All rights reserved.**

The content contained within this book may not be reproduced, duplicated or transmitted without direct written permission from the author or the publisher.

Under no circumstances will any blame or legal responsibility be held against the publisher, or author, for any damages, reparation, or monetary loss due to the information contained within this book, either directly or indirectly.

Legal Notice:

This book is copyright protected. It is only for personal use. You cannot amend, distribute, sell, use, quote or paraphrase any part, or the content within this book, without the consent of the author or publisher.

Disclaimer Notice:

Please note the information contained within this document is for educational and entertainment purposes only. All effort has been executed to present accurate, up to date, reliable, complete information. No warranties of any kind are declared or implied. Readers acknowledge that the author is not engaged in the rendering of legal, financial, medical or professional advice.

The content within this book has been derived from various sources. Please consult a licensed professional before attempting any techniques outlined in this book.

By reading this document, the reader agrees that under no circumstances is the author responsible for any losses, direct or indirect, that are incurred as a result of the use of the information contained within this document, including, but not limited to, errors, omissions, or inaccuracies.

Table of Contents

Chapter 1..8

The History of Wicca

Chapter 2..13

Why is Wicca Witchcraft So Common?

Chapter 3..17

Forms of Wicca and Wiccan traditions

Chapter 4..28

Your First Steps As a Wicca Beginner

Chapter 5..32

Want to Become a Wiccan?

Chapter 6..36

A Beginner Guide to Wiccan and Beliefs

Chapter 7..40

The Five Points of Wiccan Belief

Chapter 8..43

A Wiccan House Blessing

Chapter 9..48

Understanding The Wiccan Gods

Chapter 10..52

Things You Should Know About Wicca

Chapter 11..58

Wicca and Witchcraft

Chapter 12..**65**

Wiccan Traditions

Chapter 13..**71**

The Truth About Wiccan Sex Magic Rites

Chapter 14..**74**

Guidance for Wicca Beginners

Chapter 15..**82**

General Information for the Beginner Wicca

Chapter 16..**85**

Your Wicca Daily Devotions

Chapter 17..93

Voodoo, Wiccan and Witchcraft Love Spells

Chapter 18..99

The Wicca Calendar

Chapter 19..106

A Beginner's Guide to Wiccan Spells and Rituals

Chapter 20..116

Wicca Information, With Free Spells, Wicca Symbols and Beliefs For the Wicca Beginner!

Chapter 21..119

Top Tips For Spells

Chapter 22..................................124

3 Simple Spells For Beginners

Chapter 23..................................129

Wicca Symbols Explained

Chapter 24..................................133

Wicca Symbols and What They Can Mean to You

Chapter 25..................................135

Astrology in Wicca

Chapter 26..................................144

Witch Spells How They Work & How to Write Your Own

Chapter 27..................................153

Misconceptions About Wicca

Chapter 1

The History of Wicca

The history of witchcraft at es back to the Paleolithic about 40,000 years ago. Archaeologists have discovered cave paintings of this period depicting witchcraft in its basic form. Our ancient ancestors would not have considered themselves witches, but they used practices associated with witchcraft today.

Witchcraft evolved from that time on and was much more commonly referred to as such from before the Middle Ages. The practice of witchcraft was fundamental to many cultures of this period and was widely practiced in Europe where it is most often referenced. The emergence of Christianity as the main religion of the time would bring unspeakable misery to those who practice witchcraft.

Many of the so-called Witches of that time, who for the most part were healers who used basic herbs to treat their villages, were persecuted as a result of the edicts of

Pope John XXII in 1320. The history of witchcraft was mainly peaceful until that time, since witches were not directly sought by the Inquisition, but this edict authorized the Inquisition to pursue Wizards as well.

Estimates of those who were killed during this period range from 40,000 to 100,000, many of whom were brutally murdered for revenge or jealousy more than for the practice of witchcraft. Burning at the stake was the original method of execution, but this later changed to hanging in many areas because it was less barbaric.

Witchcraft would be practiced in secret for centuries accordingly if this treatment.

Modern practices are widely called neopaganism, although this term does not accurately represent the many varieties followed in modern times. Traditional witchcraft as a way of life with a very limited direct structure is probably the most common, but there are more irregular religious forms of witchcraft. Wicca is perhaps the best known of them and is very much a religion involving witchcraft.

During the history of witchcraft, there were established general principles governing all congregations or witches, which led to each Coven practicing the Arts in their own way, as directed by their individual direction. Solo practice is also wide and unique, always following the same beliefs.

Wiccan beliefs many people practice today can trace their ancestors to our ancient stone age past. Evidence of the beginning of Wicca's long history can be seen for the first time in the cave paintings of the Pyrenean regions of France and Spain dating back about 17,000 years. Concerned about the success of the hunt, these paintings are usually very far underground and are clearly destined to invoke the help of the Goddess Mother Earth.

A major change in the history of Wicca came with the spread of Agriculture in Europe about 10,000 years ago. Peoples ' relationship with the Earth has changed and their need for a wider range of deities to help and protect them has expanded. The trials of the elemental gods are becoming more common with the gods and goddesses of wind, rain, thunder and fertility added to the ancient sun god and moon goddess and the history of Wicca is beginning to become more familiar to us. The Ancient Gods of hunting retreated into the woods and forests and became gods of nature and the" Wild Forest" usually represented by the horned figure of Herne the hunter or the leafy green man.

As communities grew, it became necessary for a specialized priesthood to evolve. In the history of Wicca, Celtic Druids are often established as direct ancestors of today's Wiccan. Druids trained in their craft for twenty years before becoming very important and influential members of their communities. Often considered the culmination of the history of Wicca were able to move freely between tribes and kingdoms. The power of the Druids was so great that many historians now believe that the Romans brought Britain into the Empire to put an end to their influence in Gaul. With the fall of the Druids, religious beliefs returned to a more personal and disorganized level. This was the situation until the suppression of these beliefs from the middle of the first millennium by the new Christian religion.

From this moment to the present day, the history of Wicca has changed from being an openly practiced religion and by necessity has become "underground". The Latin word "pagan" simply means an inhabitant of the countryside or the rustic, the ancient ways were kept alive in rural areas by "wise women" who would have used their knowledge of magic and plant lore, to help their neighbors, and it was at this time in the history of the god and goddess That the ancient ways were kept alive in the areas

Fortunately, in the mid-twentieth century there has been a revival of interest in the old-fashioned way, with the publication in 1954 of Gerald Gardner's book "Witchcraft Today" is generally considered to be a renaissance time in the history of Wicca, to the point that today it is the 5th largest religion in the United States, with nearly 1 million active participants.

Chapter 2

Why is Wicca Witchcraft So Common?

It is said that the black magic of Wicca is the fastest growing religion among high schools and the lining in America. It is also now drilled by people from a wide range of different backgrounds, including experts as legal advisers and educators.

Wiccans practice what they call white Enchantment, which they accept is "great" and ranges from" terrible " dark enchantment.

The inspiration that pushes to engage in Wicca is not vile in any way. Included individuals must take advantage of the great "powers" of nature and lead them in a positive way. They are looking for the "ability" to have the ability to perform a great enchantment, and as a rule to locate in the same way a well-known gathering to have a place with. The amount of witch assemblies is expanding day by day. The Wiccan have great virtues as authenticity.

Books such as the Harry Potter arrangement, and Life TV shows "Buffy", "Sabrina the High School Witch", "enchanted" and other comparative shows have skyrocketed the fame of black magic Wicca, in an extraordinary way.

The term witch, Never Again is by all accounts related to a scary elderly person sporting dark and riding on a broomstick, assumed

 the appearance of attractive young women, or young high school kids.

Wiccans are not evil individuals trying to devastate the world, but tragically they are careless about the authentic idea of the forces they are benefiting from.

Wiccans have no confidence in the villain or evil presences and this is the best disaster. They do not understand that the source of the enchantment in which they dig does not yet come from the "nature" of the vile Ace of the Undetectable world of devilry. Deceitful spirits of evil spirits work diligently, attracting the unconscious into a dangerous cycle that can demolish their lives. It is only when individuals are vigorously engaged with Wicca that they discover that they begin to experience "terrible spirits", "mystical assaults", "terrible energies" and "destructive voices" in their minds apart from other things. At this point, they need to start trying out what they call "enchantment assurance."

There really are extraordinary powers of good and malice in the game room in this world and the Bible finds out what those powers are. The Bible predicts that in the last days there will be a lot of mysterious apparitions, and wandering spirits will overflow and try to deceive even the choice.

We should be extremely conscious so as not to open an inappropriate door to another world. We have to look for reality. The Wiccans trust the resurrection, but the Bible says: Hebrews 9: 27 "and as it is called to men once surprising, after that the judgment:" the Wiccans have no faith in the demon, but then the Bible shows unequivocally that it exists. Probably the most terrible thing is, however, that the Wiccans do not think they need to have a friend in need, but the Bible encourages us that Jesus Christ gave his life, in order that all may be excused, in the event that they recognize him as Lord of their lives. 1 Timothy 4: 10 " for therefore we Labor and endure reproach, for we entrust ourselves to the living God, Who Is the Savior all the same, not usually of those who accept."

The devil is fit as a violin in this world and to hurt as many honored manifestations of God as he can. In the event that you are associated with Wicca, or know someone who is, you would all be encouraged to examine both sides of the condition, and in any case think about what the Bible discovers mysterious practices and the source of their ability.

Chapter 3

Forms of Wicca and Wiccan traditions

The Wicca Rheedia

A retired British official named Gerald B. Gardner is the "grandfather", at least, of almost every new Wicca. He was cast into a clan of witches in the New Forest area of England in 1939 by a high priestess named" old Dorothy "Clutterbuck. In 1949 he wrote a novel [*High magical Aid*] about medieval witchcraft in which part of the craft practiced by this congregation was used. In 1951, the last English laws against witchcraft were repealed (mainly due to pressure from spiritualists) and Gardner published *Witchcraft Today*, which established a version of the rituals and traditions of this coven. There is a huge amount of disagreement about almost every statement I made in this paragraph.

Gardnerianism is both a tradition and a family, and lineage is a family tree. The High Priestess directs the congregation and the principles of love and trust President. We follow our pronounced book more carefully than many others, but we are free to add and improvise, as long as we keep the original.

We work sky clad, we practice linking and flogging, we are hierarchical and secret, so we are controversial. We are also controversial because we were the first-the first craft tradition in the United States and we descended from the man largely responsible for initiating the craft renaissance. So we're called the trade snobs, but I think we're as funny as anyone else; our parties are good, our jokes are bad.

Each Gardnerian clan is autonomous and is led by a high priestess who can turn to her Queen (the high priestess who formed her) for advice and advice. This maintains the lineage and creates a pool of experienced and competent leaders and teachers.

Reincarnation and the Wiccan Rede [evil, do what you want] are traditional basic tenants. Congregations are as far as possible composed of male / female pairs for balance. Most of the work is carried out with the Energy raised by the interaction of the Lord and the lady, represented by couples in the convent of dance, singing, etc.

Like many Wiccan traditions, gardnerians have three degrees. An American Gardnerian must be 3rd degree before he can become an HPS. HPS / HP are responsible for the conduct of services (circles), the training of their summoners and the conservation and transmission of Gardnerian ships. *[This material cited by Converging paths Newsletter, Kyril, Brita, & Hugh authors.]

Most of the controversies surrounding Gardnerianism question the sources of rituals and other materials, especially those that appear in the press. It is true that Gardner presented these materials as if they were directly derived from his new forestry tradition. It is clear, however, that whatever material the coven might have had when it was launched, Gerald made many changes and added a lot. Literary sources in the published book Shadows include Blake, Kipling, Yeats and Crowley. Much of the published material was written by Doreen Valiente, a member of the Coven for some time, then founder of their own groups and author of many excellent books on the craft.

Gardnerian witches undoubtedly have many materials that did not appear in the press, however, their attention to secrecy made it a distinctive line in the Wiccan social world. How many gardeners does it take to change a light bulb? It's a secret! Their high priestess will usually be called Lady, So and so and high priest, "Lord what is his name". [This is much more true in the United States than in England.]

Alessandrino Wicca

As most of all is now aware, the Alexandrian tradition is very close to Gardnerian with some small changes. (One of the most obvious is that the Alexandrians use the athame as a symbol of the fire element and the wand as a symbol of the air. Most rituals are very formal and highly indebted to ceremonial magic. It is also a polarized tradition and the sexuality of this woman/man polarity is emphasized. The ritual cycle mainly deals with the division of the year between King Holly and King oak and several ritual dramas deal with the theme die

/ resurrected god. As for the gardnerians, the High Priestess is presumably the highest authority. However, it is strange that the main spokesmen of both traditions are men. [*This material provided by Gillan]

Alexandrian Wicca is the creation of Alex Sanders (with then wife Maxine) who claimed to have been launched by his grandmother in 1933. And ' the main supporters are Janet and Stewart Fararr whose books exhibited more, if not all, of the Alexandrian tradition. Contrary to popular belief, the name Alexandrin does not refer to Alex Sanders, but to ancient Alexandria.

Although similar to Gardnerian Wicca, Alexandrian Wicca tends to be more eclectic and liberal. Some of the strict rules of Gardnerism, such as the requirement of ritual nudity, were made optional by Alexandrian Wicca.

Mary Nesnick, an American initiator in the Gardnerian and Alexandrian traditions, founded a" new" tradition called Algard.

This tradition brings together the Gardnerian and Alexandrian teachings under one banner. This was possible because of the great similarities between the two traditions.

Dianic Wicca

The Dianic craft comprises two distinct branches:

A branch, founded in Texas by Morgan McFarland and Mark Roberts, gives primacy to the goddess in her theology, but honors the Horned God as his beloved wife. Congregations are mixed, including women and men. This branch is sometimes called "Old Dianico", and there are still congregations of this tradition, especially in Texas. Other congregations, similar in Teleology but not directly descended from the McFarland / Roberts Line, are scattered throughout the country.

The other branch, sometimes called Dianic feminist witchcraft, focuses exclusively on the goddess and consists of exclusively female congregations and groups. These tend to be freely structured and not hierarchical, using consensus-the decision-making process and the simple, creative and experimental ritual. These are politically feminist groups, usually very supportive, personal and emotionally intimate. There is a strong lesbian presence in the movement, although most congregations are open to women of all orientations.

The main network is reformed congregation of the goddess, which publishes magazine "like-minded" and sponsors conferences on Dianic crafts. [*Amber K]

Celtic Wicca (Church of Wicca)

The Church of Wicca was founded by Gavin and Yvonne Frost. They offer correspondence courses in their brand of Wicca, which is sometimes called Celtic Wicca. The Church of Wicca has just begun to include a goddess in their deity structure, and has been very patrofocal as Wiccan traditions go. The Church of Wicca is called "Baptist Wicca"

Frosts call their Celtic tradition Wicca. To me, it seems more of a mix of high magic and eclectic Wicca, with a stuffed Celtic thrown in. For example, they use three circles, one in the other, salt, sulfur and herbs with runes and symbols between them instead of a circle. They also insist on a white-sleeved athame and will not have a black-sleeved athame, while all the other traditions I've heard or read about using a black-sleeved athame. It seems to me that the Wicca they practice and teach should not be called Celtic at all; but since many of them are made up or assembled from other traditions, they should also give it a fancy name; let's say freezing. If you don't have to pay for the course and you have a little extra time, it would probably be worth reading just for comparison. [*De Circé, who followed their course bycorrespondence.]

Frosts have always been a bit more public than most traditions (announcing their course in the Enquirer and similar publications), which has earned them heavy criticism in less public craft groups.

Georgian Wicca

If a word could better describe the Georgian tradition, it would be "eclectic". Although the material provided to the students was nominally Alexandrian, there was never any imperative to follow this path blindly. George Patterson (founder of tradition) has always said: "if it works, use it, if it doesn't, don't. "The newsletter was always full of contributions from people of many traditions. I've always felt that Pat's intention was to provide jump points for students and members. So, although I can claim initiation in more than one tradition, I will always consider myself " Georgian first: George is much missed, let the god-dess look at him. Brilliant Blessings, Lord Fafner.

Discordianism (Erisian)

The Discordiano or Erisiano movement is described as a "non- Prophet irreligious disorganization and claimed' the erisiana revelation is not a complicated putting disguised as a new religion but a new religion disguised as a complicated putting to Mr. 'it all

started with the *' Principia Discordia, or how I found the goddess and what I did when I found her , * a collection of articles and ideas compiled by Greg Hill (Malaclypse the younger-er). The central theme is "chaos is as important as order" as illustrated in Greyface's curse story:

Humor is at the heart of Discordianism, but Discordianism should not be dismissed as a joke. Deep experiences often accompany practice or Erisinaism. It is a penetrating game, which shows that absurdity is as valid as the world, and chaos is as valid as order. Free the practitioner from the games of order (which most have forgotten are games) to play with order or games with chaos, or both. The effects of Discordianism on an individual can be profound and incredibly liberating. [Although a large number of immature individuals played Discordianism and thus escaped any possibility of spiritual growth- gray cat * ironically*]

Chapter 4

Your First Steps as a Wicca Beginner

For a Wicca tenderfoot, you have to look as if the data is not infinite. I have a mixture of jealousy and compassion towards you! On the one hand, being a Wicca novice is energizing and revolutionary.

There is not at all such a hurry to find the old wisdom and understand how to feel and channel forces and energies into your general environment. But then I can identify as well as I remember being mastered by the amount I needed to learn and not progress. So to help you on your way to this energizing journey, here are 5 tips to get started.

1) Many Wicca tenderfoots refer to spell giving a role as one of their essential goals behind the search for confidence. In addition, there is no uncertainty as to whether it is one of the best moments and life that confirms the Wicca parties. It is not simple, and you need to understand that this is an experience that many as a method of directing "magical forces". You need to understand how to evaluate the forces that exist within

you and what your style is, and then save time for a simple week-to-week spell session to perceive how you progress.

Opt for something basic, for example, a spell to bring positive energies in the next 7 days. Check if you can take advantage of these emotions and attract the energy of others to you. This will give you an atmosphere for the energies, the spirit of the components, the potential that exists within you, and to conclude things, help you see exactly how much fun to run magic can be!

2) The 5 All-Inclusive Components are essential to trust and the nascent needs of Wicca need to start bringing these components into their lives and filling up at the first opportunity. These components are the endowments of Air, Fire, Water, Earth and soul (this speaks to you and your place on Earth). These components have various strengths and qualities, so you should start to perceive and consider them. An important element of Wicca is the belief that the energies used will return to you with several times the power, so

it is a good hope to ensure that the vitality you transmit is constantly positive. Try to start making a propensity to give something to the universe when you can, from a show of consideration to the fall of money into the box of philanthropy.

3) Look for a quiet place to play your spell work or for your intervention and reflections. It's nice to discover a place where you feel good and safe and start to be an element of a costume, in and of itself. As a Wicca student, you will only need tools for a special improvised raised area. A bowl for water, a light, incense and a little salt will regularly do the work for an essential raised area, but incorporate something individual (photo or more liked some ornaments for example) until you start to feel really comfortable.

4) Find neighborhood assets or meetings (congregations). You will be invited and started as prepared in the coven-specific methods you have chosen. Casual that you are lucky enough to have a wide range of traditions near your home at that time converse with everyone to check if you are attracted to one more

than the others. Despite this, not everyone has such extravagance, so it's also good to see you as one. For this, I suggest going on the web and participating in meetings and discussions. You will find that individuals are happy to share their insight and experience.

5) Be reasonable about what you hope to happen as a Wicca tenderfoot. You will not have the opportunity to make supernatural events, and you should not seek to twist the choice of others. In case you think these might be behind your explanations behind the need to grab Wicca, you may need to think about it a little more. You will have to consider Wicca as a comfortable and safe way of life to be set up to work there. Prices will come to you in time.

In these lines, remember this; being a Wicca tenderfoot is very similar to driving-everyone was a student once! You may feel that there is an excessive amount to take from the beginning, but take all the time you need and enjoy starting to see the potential results of what you are around. Soon, you will begin to embrace Wiccan manners as a characteristic piece of your life.

Chapter 5

Want to Become a Wiccan?

You want to be a Wiccan? Assuming the answer is yes, you'll probably already have a lot of information and you're wondering what your next step should be. Here are some things to consider and a look at what the

options are. If you're still interested in becoming Wiccan by the end, you've already taken your first step!

Why do I want to become a Wiccan?

Okay, first, a little introspection. To become a Wiccan, you must be ready to take personal responsibility. Compared to many other confessions Wiccan is relaxed and also accommodating in its values and there are very few rules to follow. However, this does not mean that you will not have commitments to fulfill because Wicca is a permanent practice. This requires the desire to learn and embrace new concepts - to improve yourself, your skills and asks you to return to the world.

You have to learn how to adopt the Wiccan Rede, one of the main rules (and as mentioned above, some rules!). Your commitment is to always take into account the well-being of others, and yourself, in your practice-" one who does not hurt, is not true". If you are sure that this is the case, then you are free to do as you like.

If I become a Wiccan, can I cast spells?

Casting spells is not essential for Wicca, but it is a wonderful activity and life affirmation that will teach you a lot about yourself. They are a wonderful way to encourage positive change-to bring true love, to you, to encourage a gift of money when you need it, etc.

It will not give you "special powers", but will allow you to reveal and use the innate powers inside. It will also teach you to respect the world around you and channel these external powers and use them for your spell work.

Do I have to join a band or a coven?

To become an experienced and responsible witch/Wiccan, it would be better to look for a local group. They will be able to teach you the ways and help you start your spiritual path. Either way, this is not always possible because you may live in a remote area or generally disapprove of your choice of faith. This does not stop you as much as you think and many Wiccan practice as solitary.

If you choose the solitary path, you can opt for a self-initiation ritual. You may want to look for one that suits you, but I think it's nice to write one for you. So it would be wise to give you some time before doing so; to familiarize yourself with Wiccan values.

What's my next step?

Your first step to becoming Wicca should be to talk to as many people about their journey as possible. This is a very personal progression and therefore, it will give you an idea of how many options there are to get you out of there. There are many online forums that you can join to do this, and you will find it warm and welcoming!

You can also try to work on the connection with nature. You will begin to open and see the divine in the world around you. This will begin to inspire you, encourage you to take the time to appreciate nature and commit to one of the basic principles of Wicca - live your life with respect. If you think you can adopt this attitude and their connection to the Earth, then you know you have what it takes.

Chapter 6

A Beginner Guide to Wiccan and Beliefs

The Wiccan are a neo-pagan religion based on nature that has formed in some divisions, for example Gardnerian, Alexandrian and eclectic Wicca.

Wicca and Black Magic are regularly used as synonyms without information or understanding of Wiccan beliefs. Wicca is the name that was received by witches naturally based on separating their religion from the well-known, much feared and abused perspective on witches as a whole. Wicca or Wicca really involves cunning. There is normally the act of black magic within religion, but not exactly for what it is for the person to choose whether that specific part of religion is directly for them.

Black magic is not only polished by Wiccan, but by many different encounters of individuals with different beliefs. It is actually welcomed by individuals within the Christian Trust, for example. Different witches, for example, traditional witches and cover witches have their own codes (belief and perspective) on how they practice their interpretation of black magic.

Wiccan beliefs focus on the essential energies of nature on Earth and in the sky above.

Their belief is exceptionally from another world and they decide to repeat the great white magic for the benefit and advancement of all included. Worshipping the deities is at the heart of their religion, God and Goddess, everything they are and everything they study. The Lord of Wiccan convictions is the Horned God, who embodies the male piece of this dictatorial religion and the Triple Goddess is the three phases of female life; Lady; Mother and hag. The Horned God is anything but a sinister God or tied to malice or Satan in any structure. It is an ancient and revolutionary iconic deity, originally from Christianity, from which Satan was born.

Wiccan beliefs express that the universe is in an impartial state of vitality. There are neither great nor terrible extraordinary powers in nature, but the way these energies are diverted decides whether black or white magic is the end result.

The beliefs of Wiccan prescribe membership in the Wiccan Rede, which are rules and a code of Conduct containing the fundamental principle "do no harm and no harm will come to you. These principles are reinforced by the Triple law also known as the law of Return, which urges its individuals "all that you transmit will return to you triple" and authorizes a great practice of lead and black magic.

The Wiccans are in any case liberal in their great deeds and incredibly wary of any bad deeds.

Wiccan's convictions do not permit the penance of living creatures or the act of dark enchantment as this explicitly denies their network and their law of three. Wiccan's beliefs incorporate recovery strategies and bring help and help using great magic spells to those who are unlucky. An accomplished repetition Witch will be all around centered around her art and have a high level of self-control, strong beliefs and information. Personalized love is seen in extraordinary majestic days.

The strict and moral occasion is a part of this religion that allows them to be available to others of various beliefs.

To describe the beliefs of Wicca and Wiccan is to recognize individuals of trust, respect, decency of heart and one with all the powers of nature.

Chapter 7

The Five Points of Wiccan Belief

Wicca is an extremely calm, pleasant and regulated perspective and life that advances unity with the heavenly and all that exists. Black magic is an otherworldly structure that cultivates the free idea and will of the individual, supports learning and understanding of the Earth and nature accordingly by confessing the heavenly nature in every living thing. One thing we live every day:

1. Wiccan Rede-injured no

2. The law of return- (otherwise known as karmic law) what you do influences what affects you.

3. The ethics of self-responsibility-we make our destiny, and define most of our "minuses". With this ethics, you tolerate karma or the "stuff" you give yourself, positive or negative.

4. The ethics of constant improvement - it changes decisively, develops

5. The ethics of tuning-tuning, the demonstration of revealing itself above godlikeness is the reason behind most Customs. In Wicca, we count on three groups of heavenly nature:

*   The divine self.

*   Different gods / forces are divine.

*   The universe itself is divine.

We started a site that consolidated our beliefs. It does not matter whether its treatment based on perfume, stones, precious stones, Tarot, sterling silver ornaments or the help of a spell we have.

Perform ceremonies appropriately adjust the intensity of the universe to your point and achieve the progressions you are looking for. Anyway, this is not the time, and the enchantment of execution does not replace helping you in a gradually common way. You need to need what you cast the spell for and you need to follow that urge. It causes in the event that you also tune in to your instinct. When we receive a spell, we will also send you a favorite stone that has been charged for you and a statement.

The stones have energies that will improve your life on many streets. Use them in contemplation, casting spells or simply passing them along with you. Bring money, fulfillment, karma, love, guarantee or recovery into your life.

Perfume-based treatment is a strategy by which the use of certain fundamental oils is consolidated or used alone to advance recovery and prosperity by applying the oils legitimately to our body or from inner breathing.

The intensity of the fragrance is something that cannot be denied, but a large amount of time is something that many of us seem not to pay attention to. Some perfumes can advance the repair of our body, psyche and soul and also to help improve overall prosperity from our psychological point of view.

Chapter 8

A Wiccan House Blessing

Perhaps the best part of repeating Wicca is that it allows its experts to give favors to other people, themselves and their environment. What exactly does that mean? All in all, just as the sanctuary cleric or priest can say a petition for the benefit of their assembly in order to gain a sense of prosperity and security, a witch can do much of the equivalent. However, witches do not accept that they need contact between themselves and the Divine. Therefore, they are able to enjoy this impressive vitality and drive its positive impact on their home, loved ones.

For example, from one of these types of Endowments, this article will reveal the procedure that a witch can take to perform a simple favoring house, to present the house with a sense of prosperity and friendliness.

The Banal Game

The initial segment of the purge or gift anywhere, whether it's Your Home, Office or even your carport, is to physically clean the place. Anyone who is even a little familiar with Feng Shui will reveal to you that the ailment and wreck are exceptionally problematic for the progression of vitality in your home. Despite the obstruction of positive vitality progression in your condition, mess really adds cynicism to your space.

That said, the initial step towards a decent home is to have an impeccable home

The Materials

The types of materials used in a deep gift will change from individual to individual, depending on their tradition and individual tastes. However, usually there are used tools with which most witches are extremely familiar.

They are:

- Incense purges, e.g. sage or incense
- Holy Water
- A melodic element, for example, a music box, a drum or a singing bowl
- broom

- White candles enabled

Blessing

When the Witch and the other member are ready to start, the Witch will launch a custom circle (a simple insurance service) that complements the entire house. As an important aspect of this service, The Witch will use incense or smirch stick to rub and foster the Home promote members. In this way, the Witch can recite something like this:

"With the forces of fire and air, I cleanse you from pessimism and do you good for these rituals"

When all limbs are so purified, the individual who leads the House moves from space to stand with incense, carrying smoke into each of the alcoves and crevices. As they do, the Witch will present a serenade, for example,

"With the forces of fire and air, I wash this space and exile any antagonism from this house

When this is over, the Witch at that time moves from space to live with a diffuser of holy water (often with a limited amount of salt broken in it), sprinkle all the pieces of each room. The Serenade for this piece of the procedure can go something like this;

"With the forces of water and earth, I sanctify this space and welcome the energies of prosperity, well-being and Concord in this house"

Now it is normal for a witch to pick up a melodic instrument or a similarity with it. It could be a drum, ringing, singing bowl, or even a tuning fork. They will move from space to the room playing their instrument, imagining the clamor of the instrument that separates the squares of negative vitality in the House. A serenade could be a piece of this progression, as agitation and representations are the essential element of this progression.

When the house is cleaned as such, the Witch can direct an ever- widening habit to welcome pleasant energies into the house to maintain the flow of positive vitality they have accumulated. It is really based on how comfortable the occupants of the House are with such a custom.

This is just one of the various types of gifts out there that witches can openly present to other people. It is crucial that the gift of this kind occurs and has an exceptionally positive effect on people who experience it. No doubt this is a stripped-down record of what a house of purification and foster entails.

Despite a favoring home, Wiccans out there perform amenities for an assortment of reasons. The potential results are enormous. Some examples of the different types of gifts are

A healing custom for a companion who has fallen ill

A safety habit before a long and difficult hike or flight experience

Offer a defensive spell to a loved one who is in the army

Make a gift to get married recently for the long and optimistic wedding the decay can continue forever...

Chapter 9

Understanding the Wiccan Gods

Wicca is a polytheistic religion, which means it has more than incomparable unfading being. Truth be told, there are two Wiccan (what we would call) divine beings.

The first is the Goddess, otherwise called the Triple Goddess and Mother Earth. The second is a divinity who is known as the triple horned god and is periodically alluded to as "Lucifer", which in Latin signifies "light conveyor". (Not to be mistaken for the Christian fallen angel).

Both the Goddess and the Triple-Horned God are said to be distinctive in polarities, which enables them to commend one another. This makes the God and Goddess the Wiccan rendition of the yin and yang; their disparities enable them to be joined together, where one is feeble the other is solid. The Goddess is the moon and the Triple Horned God is the sun.

In the Wiccan religion, the divinities are not seen as genuine individuals, yet Cosmic forces that show inside any physical being and can be reached through enchantment, customs and celebrations.

The Triple Goddess

The Triple Goddess is alluded to by a wide range of names and furthermore portrayed as a triadic god: the lady goddess, Mother goddess and the hag goddess. Different names that the Triple Faced Goddess is known as include:

Mother earth The moon Goddess Diana Wicca.

Most Wiccans see the "goddess" as the most significant of the two divinities. The God is seen as her associate, the sparkle inside the Goddess that makes her motivation. This shows in the structure of cutting edge covens; as a rule, the leader of a coven is female, speaking to the Goddess as the essential power.

To Wiccans, the Goddess speaks to: virginity, richness and - generally significant of all - knowledge. Current researchers have found and demonstrated that divinities known as "triple horned goddesses" were adored in the British Isles in antiquated and early Medieval occasions, however it's as yet not known whether these references are to a similar god as the Wiccan "triple goddess" of today.

The Triple Horned God

Normally, most wiccans allude to their God as 'the triple horned god", however he can be known by different names, including: Lucifer, the Devil and Satan. These names have nothing to do with the Christian philosophy of "the fallen angel", the leader of the black market; the Wiccan God is tranquil, yet these names have been adjusted by Wiccans as an affirmation of noteworthy occasions when wiccans were blamed for black magic and hanged by the neck. After some time, the Christian criticism of the Wiccan God as a "fallen angel" has slipped into the Wiccan language itself.

Every so often the Triple Horned God is known as the green man, because of his portrayal of normal world. This is proceeded by another equivalent word; the Sun God.

The God is commended in numerous Wiccan celebrations, including Litha (better referred to non-Wiccans as the late spring solstice). The Solstice is, truth be told, especially essential to Wiccans; celebrated on the longest day of the year - June 21st - it speaks to the God giving light and vitality to the Goddess.

A few wiccans accept that there are two substances to the God: the "Oak King" and "Holly King"; one guidelines over Winter and Spring and the other Autumn and Summer.

The Triple Horned God speaks to the wild, sexuality, chasing and the cycle of life.

Chapter 10

Things You Should Know About Wicca

If you start along your spiritual path, it can sometimes be very intimidating or even frightening. When you seek knowledge, who should you believe? I will offer wise advice "do not believe everything you read, but always follow your institution. "If something is wrong or that little voice in your head says "not at all," then listen. Here are some real facts about Wicca / witchcraft that can help you on your way to universal truths and enlightenment.

1.   Wicca is a true religion. Wicca is a religion protected by the Constitution of the United States. There are Wiccans who openly serve in the U.S. Army. There are many variations on how to practice Wicca. Wicca is an Earth-based religion. We believe in the elements, God and Goddess and different types of supernatural beings and much more.

2.   Wicca is a structured religion, but there are no extreme directives. Yes, there are some basic rules that most Wiccans follow, but nothing is really etched in

stone. Each person who practices Wicca has his own guidelines and rules, as well as his beliefs, customs, works of spells, practices and deities with which he prefers to work. As you continue your studies on Wicca, it is up to you to decide what is right for you and what your true spiritual needs are.

3. Most Wiccans follow a moral and ethical code. If someone you know says he is Wiccan, they follow the Wiccan Rede and practice black magic. This statement is an oxymoron. When they practice black magic, they work with dark and dangerous entities like demons. When someone plays with black magic, they can be extracted in the dark even before they realize they have been captured. Wicca imitates the beliefs of the Amerindians in such a way that all living things are sacred. In Wicca, many believe in Wiccan Rede. One line from Wiccan's reading States: "if you don't hurt anyone, do whatever you want. Most Wiccan do not cast spells that will harm another person.

4. Is there an afterlife in Wicca? Some Wiccan believe that there is an afterlife, others do not. Most Wiccan believes in reincarnation.

Gerald Gardener wrote that summer the Earth is a place of rest for souls until they are reborn. Within Wicca, most believe that psychics and psychics can reach through the great division and talk to our lost loved ones and other omniscient and omniscient entities.

5. If you decide that Wicca is where your spirituality is located, will it be time to decide whether you will live an open life like Wiccan or stay in the broom closet so to speak? It is necessary to keep in mind that there is still a plethora of narrow views on the Wicca religion. Here are some questions you should ask yourself before deciding to live an open, honest and free Wiccan lifestyle.

Am I financially independent? If your parents still pay their bills, then the answer is no. Do you want to cut emotionally and financially? If your parents practice Christians, maybe they do. Always think before acting.

Can I lose my job? In most cases, you shouldn't, but it's still a very rough terrain for the average Wiccan. You ask me, Can I prove that I was fired because of my religious beliefs? If so, then by all means go out. For most Wiccan, this is not the case in their reality. It is up to the employee to provide evidence or discrimination. Take the test if you decide to go this way.

6. Wiccans don't worship the devil. The devil is in the dark. The belief of traditional Wicca is that of light. In traditional Wicca there is no gray area. Many people assume that Wiccans and witches adore dark entities and they will turn you into a toad or give you a nasty Juju or cast a curse on you. Let's say you have a ruler on a 12-inch scale to be the ones who worship Satan / the devil until the end of the twelfth inch is where Wiccans would be listed. Wiccans don't worship dark entities or the devil.

7. New witches should use other spells and rituals. Well, the truth is yes and no. For many new witches, it seems impossible for them to write their own rituals and spells. If you don't feel confident writing your own spells

or rituals, then you should find a ritual or spell in a book or online and make it your own. A very important aspect of becoming a Wiccan is that you understand that you are capable, you can succeed at whatever you put your effort and mind into. If something seems right to you, but others say that it is not right or will not work, then you should look at all aspects and then do what you think is right. A great philosophy here is "for self to be true."You need to feel comfortable and did not wear uncertain and random. Spirituality comes from within your magic comes from powers and your determination comes from your solid heart. Never doubt yourself or your beliefs because these things make us tangible, make us all eternal. They make us who we are.

8. Should you do solitary worship and magic or would you be more comfortable in an alliance? Are you more comfortable alone? Does your magic feel stronger when you are alone or intensifies when there are other people involved? For many joining a coven helps because they can finally be around others who share their path and have similar experiences and ideas as they do. For some, it seems that the structure of a pact

feels very comfortable. For others who adhere to a pact, it feels restrictive and chaotic for them. Only you can answer these questions yourself.

9. For many new Wicca practitioners, they are under the misconception that they have to spend thousands of dollars on ritual craft tools and spells. This is simply not true. When you are a beginner, you can use objects around your home. Be sure to clean all the tools that you decide to use.

This will release all negative energies and amplify the effectiveness of your rituals or spells. If you want to simplify your ritual spells and crafts, why not work with candle spells or seal spells? Both can be easily hidden if you are not out yet. They also offer minimal material cost and can help you build your practical knowledge of magic on a shoe chain budget..

Chapter 11

Wicca and Witchcraft

You can be exceptionally confused with the cutting-edge thoughts present today. In fact, many people are so engaged in their lives that they do not try to think about the origin of these traditional and avant-garde views. Today, it develops, for example, the religion, the problems of government, combat, and even the web all started a place, and it is significant that individuals know a little about the historical context of something before using it fully as a piece of their daily existence adjust. Take the example of Witchcraft and Wicca: while a large number of people would probably join these two in similar territory, for example black magic and spells with the intermittent supernatural device, for example the voodoo doll, you might be shocked that Wicca is really a religion and black magic is really a religion.

What is Wicca?

Wicca is truly an advanced agnostic religion, and focuses on an increasingly calm, pleasant and regulated lifestyle. This is really an image of pre-Christian belief, which is usually the way our ancestors lived and revered. It is known to be one of the most experienced conviction frameworks known on the planet today, and is mostly frowned upon by the advanced Christian Church in light of the solid impact of enchantment and another world that was commonly present in practices.

Like most belief structures that are mostly disapproved of by Christians, Wiccan practices have a deeper meaning than that, which is increasingly focused on love for divine beings and accepted goddesses, as well as fixation on nature. Wicca is initially known as "the specialty of the wise", and the general acts of which include the search of the equality of man and nature and the understanding that man and the various components that man has made are only components of nature.

History of Wicca

Before the era of black magic and spells, current devices, for example, candles and voodoo dolls, as well as the general belief that black magic is intelligent, Wicca is commonly known to be a framework of belief in Ireland, Scotland and Wales. It was advanced in the' 50s and ' 60s by Gerald Gardener. At that time, Wicca was originally called "Witch clique "and" BLACK magic", which essentially clarifies the current low appreciation of the term Wicca. The disposition of conviction is a solid pre-Christian birth and pursues a pre-eminent trust in nature and the other world and the pleasant relationship of man with the components of nature.

Is Wicca safe?

Wicca, as well as all the different frames of conviction and other world, is perfectly protected. In the event that you move beyond the set of black magic and spells that are firmly subsidiary with religion, you may find that they focus on a pleasant connection between them and nature. It is not natural to hurt something or someone and, therefore, do not hope that Wiccan will hurt anyone. The various representations of black magic and

Wicca do accept the general population to be a religion of admirers of the left, who remain inactive, but to throw insults and hexes against one another using spells, causing damage to people using different devices of another world, for example, a voodoo doll, to, or participate in is incredibly far from reality, since Wicca is not involved in any of this. They recognize the perfect, but do not make themselves known as rigorous pioneers to be followed by individuals in search of another world, nor do they guarantee to worship Satan or evil spirits. Satan and the presences of evil are made only by Christians and are mistakenly linked to Wicca and witchcraft.

What does Wiccan accept?

Similarly, as with several strict sentencing frameworks, Wicca has a sentencing agreement that continues:

As For Theology. Wicca is basically a duo theistic religion and has faith in a God and goddesses considered inverse and polar deities that examples of the power of life in nature are essentially.

Like the afterlife. For the most part, they do not trust the afterlife and emphasize power over current life. However, some Wicca professionals have confidence in the Renaissance

Speaking Of Magic. Enchantment for a Wiccan is basically a power of nature and keeping in mind that many Wiccan have no idea how black magic and spells work, they trust nature.

As for morality. They pursue a difficult code of "hurt none", which essentially expresses that Wicca does not allow hurting all living beings.

As for the five elements. They trust the four components: Air, Water, Earth and fire, with a fifth component to adjust and unite the four that is known as Ether or spirit

Wicca and witchcraft

As recently expressed, there is a general error of judgment regarding Wicca and witchcraft. Most current ideas are much more accustomed to the possibility that witchcraft focuses on how to be a witch with more developed clients learning adoration spells and other spells that are sinister and hateful in nature. Due to the well-known appearance of television and cinema, Wicca has become synonymous with witchcraft, most often without exchanging both thoughts. Topical is, witchcraft is however an insignificant piece of the Wiccan religion, and it is a narrow belief that illuminates an individual's understanding of the Earth and nature that attests and perceives heavenly nature in every living being. Basically, it teaches people that if external powers matter, they do not settle in our being and, therefore, they should not be blamed for everything that happens independently. It shows a must for our activities, thus ensuring a friendly harmony between land and nature.

Wicca and witchcraft perceive power or nature and at the same time the devices that nature gives us. The set of various plants, creatures and tolls that can be obtained from them, for example, tonics, mixtures and different inventions can be used to cure known diseases and known diseases of man. Wicca and black magic perceive the intensity of nature and their deep convictions allow them to work amicably with nature for a pleasant equalization of life.

The most important thing about Wicca and witchcraft is their confidence in the deity in every way, as recently expressed. The framework of conviction focuses on working cordiality between each living being with all the Revolutionary components of Earth, Air, Fire and water with the other world holding them all together. Wicca is not a clique and does not show an individual how to be a witch or different procedures such as spells or Wiccan spells to cast hexagons to others to hurt them. They draw their ability from within to create harmony with each other and with nature.

Chapter 12

Wiccan Traditions

For some of us, Wicca is a solitary religion, something we have taught ourselves through groups, books or even the Internet. If you grew up in a Wiccan family or started traditionally with a coven, it is important to understand all the Wiccan traditions.

The Wicca Gardeners

The traditional way of Gerald Gardener honors Cernunnos as the Lord and Aradia as the lady. This Wicca path is formal with degrees of worship and sky clad initiation with congregations that have no more than thirteen members in each. The congregations are led by a high priestess with a high priest. Gardeners are not too impressed by self-initiation to other forms of Wicca because they believe that it takes a witch to make a witch.

Alessandrino Wicca

Founded in the 60s by Alex and Maxine Saunders, Alexandrian Wicca is a formal, structured and neo-gardener tradition. The Gardenerian and Alexandrian Wicca are considered classic Wicca.

Traditional British Wicca

This type of Wicca is similar to Gardenerian Wicca, even formal and structured, but it also mixes Celtic deities and spirituality.

Celtic Wicca

Celtic Wicca incorporates Celtic deities and goddesses with spirituality, green witchcraft and fairy magic.

Dianic Wicca

This tradition is centered on the goddess Diane who does not include the gods. Dianic Wicca is often considered a feminist, even lesbian, although there are male Dianic witches. This path does not require initiations.

Faery Wicca

This Irish tradition is similar to Celtic Wicca with an emphasis on green witchcraft and fairy magic.

Teutonic Wicca

Teutonic Wicca incorporates the gods, symbolism and practices of the Nordic tradition, including Germanic and Nordic cultures.

Family Traditions

Generations of witches who have their own secret practices and traditions.

Oxymorphic Groups

Satanic Wiccan and Christian Wiccan are not Wiccan whether they mean good or not. This is a contradiction in terms

Although some witches believe that each individual must be taught the craft by a living relative before being considered a witch, a hereditary, however, believe that being a witch can be inherited from a grandfather who may or may not live. The natural gift of witchcraft seems to skip a generation, in many cases. There are countless reports of young witches receiving spiritual messages from their ancestors showing a guide on the path of witches or discovering information indicating that an ancestor is a witch.

Paganism

Paganism covers many confessions, one of which is Wicca. Wiccans respect others in their beliefs and appreciate freedom of worship for all. Wiccans are polytheists who incorporate various gods and goddesses into their rituals. Most witches believe in reincarnation, hence the representation of seasons, birth, death and rebirth. Some Wiccan believe that we rest in Summerlands before being reincarnated. Summerlands is the place where we are reunited with our families and loved ones.

Wiccans don't believe in hell or The Devil. Wiccan chooses to abstain from negativity by being positive. We hold an individual responsible for his wrongdoing.

Many witches honor the Lord Horned God, the Lord of Animals, The Lord Silvano of greenwood. He is also known as Pan, Herne or Cernunnos, a man with horns who is a great God of herds and fertility.

Some witches believe in Angels, some fairies, and some even believe in Dragons. Each to his own.

Different Traditions

Different traditions you may experience include:

Celtic Wicca, which underscores the enchantment and recuperating capacities of natural spirits, little persons, pixies, plants, and minerals.

Asatru (Northern Way) in view of the Norse pantheon and including Old Norse dress for custom work.

Pictish, which is a singular Scottish nature tradition. Strega, that steps traditions going back to fourteenth century Italian lessons.

While not a total rundown, these depictions unquestionably should give you a thought of the assortment characteristic in the realm of Wicca.

Chapter 13

The Truth About Wiccan Sex Magic Rites

Most of the public disapproved of sexual intercourse as part of worship. The Catholic Church finds sexual rites too carnal in nature, and has no connection to attaining Divinity and spiritual growth.

However, in Wicca, sexual rites have always been considered a divine union of God and Goddess. They call this the great rite, and it is mainly performed by insiders of the third degree. The great rite often characterized the unity of two opposite deities into one omnipotent source of energy.

In addition, the grand rite symbolizes fertility and produces a large amount of energy between two participating parties. The great rite can be real or symbolic. Some congregations use their magical instruments, the anthamus and the chalice to involve the Union of God and the goddess. Traditional congregations, however, still practice sexual magic rites to create a more intense magical power between the Union of spirits exercising the ritual.

It is dangerous that people from different spiritual horizons find the ancient Magic abusive and immoral. For Wiccan, this is a sacred act, not everyone in a particular congregation can perform the true great rite. As mentioned above, only priests and priestesses who have gained a lot of experience with rituals and magic can perform it.

They have a deeper understanding behind the sexual relationship that will shine between them. There should be no sexual attraction among the initiates who will participate in the grand rite. Yes, sexual intercourse is an experience, in which humans get pleasure, but in Wicca it is much more. Sexual rite is a ritual in which love emanates from those who participate in it. This positive energy comes from separate individuals, and at the top of the act it is united into a single heap of cosmic energy.

Although the act of the great rite has already been explained, There are still those who consider it inappropriate. Today's Wiccans have a hard time explaining these rituals to unbelievers. Wiccan are spiritual people who believe that the main purpose of Wiccan spells and magic's is to harness large amounts of energy and turn them into positive manifestations and results. Sex is still considered a taboo even for the most westernized individuals, and the idea of a show sex as a religious activity is still a big NO-NO for most people.

It will probably take time for all mankind to understand the sacredness of the great rite. For now, Wiccans are always positive that one day people will appreciate the symbolism behind the ritual and find beauty, and not the vulgarity of sex as a sacred human activity.

Chapter 14

Guidance for Wicca Beginners

If you are going to start a trip on the way to Wicca, it is worth knowing what you will need to get started. This is designed to help you as a Wicca beginner guide to help you start your spiritual journey. Although this is not a complete guide for Wicca beginners, it is a good start.

The first thing that every witch should learn and understand is the five elements. The four basic elements are Earth, Water, Fire and wind. The Fifth Element is mentioned in various ways, including void, akasha and spirit. These elements represent all the physical aspects of our experience in this physical form. The Fifth Element is the aspect of us that connects and connects, and uses, these other elements. Everything consists of water, earth, fire, wind or a combination of these elements. You need to know more about these elements if you want to develop a form of power.

The next thing everyone on the road has to earn is a bookstore. It is useful for anyone on a spiritual path to have a teacher, and books are the fastest and easiest way to get these teachers.

Of course, people can follow the path on their own, however, one or some good teachers is indispensable to significantly speed up the process.

Any good Wicca beginner's guide will also tell you that an understanding of plants, herbs, minerals and colors is also essential. They are used in many spells, and each has its own abilities. A good knowledge of plants and herbs is especially essential. This is what the original Wiccan had a great understanding of. In fact, many women were burned at the stake because of their understanding of plants and their naturally healing and useful abilities.

These aspects alone in this Wicca beginner's guide will keep you very busy for years, however, if you are going to be a serious professional, you need to know and understand festivals and ritual practices as well. There are four major, and four minor holidays throughout the year.

Wicca amateurs have a long, energizing and exciting voyage in front of them, - a way overflowing with more noteworthy information and another lifestyle. With such a great amount ahead, it is no big surprise that individuals can get themselves somewhat lost and overpowered. On the off chance that you are sufficiently fortunate to live approach a gathering or coven that you can join and be guided by then you will as of now be well on your way to your new way of life. Nonetheless, for some Wicca novices it isn't as basic as that. Topography to friends and family's very own strict convictions may keep you from getting together with others and straightforwardly proclaiming your new course.

However, you ought to never feel blocked from this superb religion nor obstructed in your capacity to tail it. There is an abundance of data out there to gain from and nothing should keep you away from figuring out how to respect and become at one with your general surroundings. In any case, seeing as this is the thing that regularly confounds the Wicca tenderfoot in any case, here are a few thoughts and fundamental clarifications to kick you off and spark your interest for additional!

What Is Wicca?

It's close to home what and each Wiccan will give you an alternative account of why they accept and what they have brought into their lives. Every Wiccan will have an adoration for the Earth and its widespread components. Water, air, fire and Earth will come to talk about magnificence, collaboration and ability for every little Wicca girl. It is connected with perception, direction and association with the Earth and its rich contributions - the blessings of Mother Nature. You will move and change in the seasons and the totality of The Associated celebrations. Most of all, Wicca speaks of harmony and happiness.

Why is it a religion?

Although it is far from being a religion in the structure that many individuals see a religion should take, Wicca is a religion because it was obtained from paganism. It assumes comparable images, paintings of conviction and, of course, deities and goddesses. It's not prescriptive as many religions are and Wicca won't reveal you how to continue your life, but it helps you understand your general environment and understand the motivation behind Life.

What is the distinction between Wicca and Black magic?

Sometimes you will discover contradictory answers to this request, however, as a student of Wicca, the subtleties of this should not concern you to the extreme. For the most part, Wicca is the strict piece of the way of life and individuals who practice it allude to themselves as Wicca or Wiccan instead of witch. They are required to be a piece of a Saturday, or picking up and complying with several rules. Anyway, the name Wicca was aware of recognizing it from the shame related to black magic and many parts of Wiccan's and witch's life are basically the same as. Terms can be interchangeable.

The Wiccan Rede

Wicca is a quiet and gentle lifestyle that allows you to consider. As a result, childish, manipulative or vile expectations are especially hated. A small minority of Wicca lovers take on a plot as they seek control over others, but it will soon go beyond one of the few standards, the Wiccan Rede - "harm no one, do as you wish." This implies that you are largely allowed to try how best you think to make sure you seize the world's ability for good as opposed to hurting or hurting others. This leads us to the overlap of Law 3 which expresses that everything you do will return to your most innovative Times. At the end of the day, be careful with what you want!

Should I worship a deity or deity?

It is not yet an important remarkable piece of the belief system and history. Similarly, they must be understood as an important aspect of male and female love. Many Wiccan will devote themselves to a

lonely God while they feel a solid taste and can relate to specific qualities. Yet Gods and goddesses can be called upon to help you in your work. As a Wicca student, it might be helpful to include any number that might be allowed in your ceremonies to see you feel specific favoritism.

Will I need to perform spells?

Nope. Not all Wiccans trust casting spells, so you shouldn't feel obligated to do so. In any case, in case you discover you have an ability here anyway, you'll discover a lot of data on spells for Wicca lovers until you get to the stage where you compose your own!

Is this A Sacred Scripture that I must submit?

The main book from which the Wiccan work is a book of Shadows and is usually an exceptionally close thing to home. A Coven may have a commune to work with, but normally you will have your own. This is a place to compose your spells, take notes and mention objective facts. It does not matter if there was even a "real" or an Old Book Of Shadows, a focal book from which to work, this is a point discussed fervently. Despite this, no one has proven to exist.

Whatever your goal behind being a Wicca novice, I am sure you will discover your advanced and educated life as one of us who chose this way for a number of reasons! You will find that there are the same number of approaches to continuing with a Wiccan lifestyle as there are Wiccan in order to enjoy every day your own adventure and another world.

Chapter 15

General Information for the Beginner Wicca

Very well, it can be difficult nowadays and time to give meaning to what religion to be, not to mention how to practice and study. In our Western culture, Christianity wins, and this makes great quality data on different religions elusive. In addition, the way he did not like to be a novice Wicca expert. In case you have chosen to be a Wicca professional Apprentice, these general data should help you get started.

The excellence of Wicca or an agnostic is the opportunity to va. The only idea is that you can do whatever you want, as long as it does not hurt anyone. Currently, this does not mean that you need to take the drug or what you want. On a deeper level, you need to build the ability to perceive how everything affects every other person. This ultimately makes it the requirement for you to build a deep awareness of others ' expectations about your life, your activities, and how the two impacts each other. This is a very important element to understand when you are a nascent Wicca professional.

The next step to consider while turning into a novice Wicca expert is to sit back and wonder if you really need to take the time and resolve to study and practice. I will be simple and in advance with you, Wicca sets aside clusters of efforts to get informed and learn. There are herbs, plants, energies, components, images, usual devices, rocks, shades, spells, ceremonies themselves, occasions, congregations and many other data that you should set aside the effort to discover and understand.

There is no shine on it, turning into an experienced Wicca newborn girl takes a lot of time and vitality to get a true understanding of black magic and the totality of goods there. Chances are that you will go through all the time on Earth and just manage a small Division, All Things Considered, you should be happy to make the dedication on the chance that you really want to turn into an experienced Wicca Apprentice. You may be one of those people who know certain things and who claim to be a Wiccan, but I have no respect for these types of individuals. Learn on the basis that it is necessary, not on the basis that it is necessary to try to be fresh for others.

When you are ready to become a witch, Wiccan, agnostic, or Wicca learner specialist, or whatever you want to call it, you need to discover someone who can encourage what you have to accomplish regarding the process of information and advancement. Discover the instructors who can give you the general tour and take you step by step through the road to transformation into an inexperienced Wicca witch or expert.

Chapter 16

Your Wicca Daily Devotions

Many people wonder exactly how your thoughts and emotions are concentrated to bring love into your life (for example), can actually make true love happen. This interaction between energies is where your faith in a higher power comes to play in Wicca witchcraft.

There are mysterious forces at work when you put your targeted thoughts and emotions to work. Whatever your specific beliefs, there are things in this world that challenge our logic and understanding. If you are like me, you have the feeling that there is "something about me" - sometimes even protect yourself from harm.

No matter your specific magical path, you will soon begin to understand that this "higher power" has some control over the interaction of your magical energy with the events of your life and the world.

The kernel you can't ignore in your witchcraft path

There are many things involved in being a witch, no matter what specific path you follow. Some of them change depending on your path (which I go into detail in my home academy), but there is one "fundamental" thing you need to follow.

This "core" is where you draw all your power-all your magic energy. And neglecting it will grind your work from magic spells to a brutal stop. Nothing will work without this basic connection.

This core I keep talking about is your connection to nature-first of all. I'm not saying that you need to move around the forest and build an improvised hut from pine branches. But you need to devote yourself to nature and try to expose yourself every day.

It can be as simple as finding a special tree in your garden and spending time next to it a few times a week (as I show you in the Daily Devotional nature later in this book).

You need to understand that you come from nature - and also the energy you control. Connecting to nature on a weekly basis will increase your connection with nature and allow you to tap into its hidden energy more easily.

Think of nature as your protector and your giver of special powers. Don't you know that someone special, like your best friend, you? Likewise, ignoring nature- Your Protector, your giver of special powers-would amount to completely "giving up" your magical powers.

Magic Tidbit #1: please, for the sake of this beautiful world in which we live, take care of yourself to help protect nature. Support all efforts to preserve nature throughout the world, and do your part to keep our world beautiful.

So keep an eye on daily devotional nature later on to find out how to strengthen your connection with nature to have better success with your magic and magic work.

Finally, as you read this book - and your magical works beyond- always keep in mind your connection with nature. If you pay attention and maintain your connection, nature will allow you to bring your dreams into your life. It will allow you to create your own miracles, do not forget about it.

When you walk a magical path, your success depends on your ability to center the charged energies and send them into the universe to get what you want.

If you ignore your association with Magic vitality, it will weaken, as Will your ability. They are especially important for the Wiccans student.

"Daily commitments" are things you constantly do to strengthen the ability to control your inner magical vitality. A respectful routine increases vitality from day to day, several times.

Consider daily prayers as short ceremonies of vitality. They strengthen your association and also bring positive energies into your life.

Regardless of anything else, you need to choose a normal one that is directly for you - and the queue every day!

You can do all your chosen prayers, one after another, or you can spread out as the day progresses. Find out something that works in your program and queue.

Your prayers can be what bring a positive feeling to your heart. It may very well be something as simple as making newspaper passages in your book of Shadows every night read before. In your book of shadows, look at where negative examples are an important part of your life, and work to develop positive examples in your psyche - and in the Book Of Shadows.

Another "smaller than normal" habit that you can pursue is to spend a few moments in any case breathing, contemplating and imagining positive things to create a positive vitality in your life. You can also use the practice of reflection that I have already given you in this book.

Here is an overview of a few moments of silence that you can do every day. You do not need to do each of them, but choose the ones that usually feel good with:

Respectful morning alarm clock Interface with Gentleman and Lady

Interfacing with divine and Infinite Energy

Welcome devotions to the spirits or elements around you Interface with nature and Mother Earth

Record

Blessing Of Food Devotion Relaxing

Contemplation Performance Exercises Play with energy

Keep in mind, none of the quiet moments you should escape by yourself. Also, you should never be in a circumstance where you are

"afraid" of doing them. You need to anticipate them, so be sure to select the ones that work best for you.

Most of the above quiet moments are obvious, and you can "do" these prayers as you wish. There are no "immovable directives" as you do your quiet moments day after day. (I expose some of them in the witchcraft Academy box)

For now, I will guide you through the simple but revolutionary" play with energy" day by day reverence.

Sit in a pleasant position and start the practice of contemplation on the nuts and bolts in this book. When you have fallen into the softening phase of breathing, open your eyes.

Take your hands, palms and rub them vigorously together. As you do, start calling the vitality around you in your body. Keep your hands in front of you, palms face to face, from twelve to eighteen chills of your face. It works best if you have a solid and boring foundation towards the path you face.

Focus first on your hands and send the vitality of your body through the palms. The moment you feel that the flow is large and solid, you simply move your concentration beyond your hands, to a point on the base beyond them. Would you be able to see the ethereal and undefined vitality among the palm trees?

This may require some investment for you to see, but to continue working on it, you. When you can see vitality in it, focus on making it more beautiful and darker, expanding flows and reducing flows. Keep playing with vitality all the time, until you settle for how to control it to do what you need to do.

When you have reached this point, start playing more vitality. Structure it into a ball, attach to the hands and separate them, seeing the ball change in size and strength.

How do you get each other's block (more days, no minutes!), try different shapes and sizes. Play with vitality and adjust with its reality. This is a similar vitality you use to launch magic. Seeing it in a

strong structure, that there is always an ethereal quality, strengthens your conviction and significantly increases your degrees of vitality.

Chapter 17

Voodoo, Wiccan and Witchcraft Love Spells

There are many types of Love Spells: Voodoo, Wiccan, witchcraft, among others. Why are not these "loves"? How are they different?

Voodoo and Wicca are religions. We can refer to a religion as a set of beliefs and worship of gods or deities. That is why magical ritual practices such as invocation (calling a deity in itself) and evocation (calling an entity in presence) tend to be part of these magical religions. So, voodoo and Wiccan love spells are made according to certain beliefs and deities.

In fact, in some cases, voodoo and Wiccan Spells For Love are only offered to their deities in exchange for their desire. Herbs, stones, crystals, etc., in them are used to attract and appeal to a specific deity or deity.

Witchcraft is not a religion (although many consider it one). Spells of witchcraft for love do not necessarily imply Divinity. This system is simply after the result.

I want to point out that the love spell does not need to involve the deities to be effective. In this case, the charmer uses his psychic abilities to change reality in the higher planes that are reflected in the physical plane. This is what the hermetic law "as above so below" refers to. This is the principle of magic.

Perhaps you have lived or heard about people who are able to see the future in dreams. They were able to do this by traveling-usually unconscious-through the upper floors before it reflected on the physical plane.

How does all this affect the results? After all, that's all that matters. Personally, I noticed that the use of deities in my spells "gives" to each other. The results tend to come a little faster and with" bonus" benefits. It seems that the deities, knowing how to bring the best results. On the other hand, the use of deities in spells can nullify them if their purpose does not agree with the deity involved in them. So, a charmer must know what he is doing; with what deities to work and when to work with them.

This shouldn't be a problem for a professional pitcher as he should have learned this in his "novice phase" a long time ago. The only difference between Voodoo, witchcraft and Wiccan Love Spells is how they are expressed. Therefore, if done right, one of them will bring the positive results you are looking for.

Wiccan and black magic spells - is there a contrast between the two? The answer to this question is yes and no! Both traditions share similar roots and, therefore, hybrids of many points of view. In both cases, you will also consider an exchange where the partitioning line is located. So if you're hoping to characterize the two, here's a look at the two similarities of Wiccan / black spells to help you in your spell work.

Differences Between Wiccan Spells / Witchcraft

The contrasts between Wiccan spells and Black Magic are usually found in the differentiation between Wiccan traditions and black magic itself. Wicca pursues to a greater extent a structure as it is a religion, and it is gradually typical for adherents to be an individual of a coven or a gathering. Here they will begin and prepare to perform spells and ceremonies in the manner of the traditions of this convent. Witches are destined to be alone, but this does not avoid the likelihood that they will come together to exchange meetings and work together.

Wiccan also regularly engages with deities or goddesses as a feature of their trust. This is because of the pagan idea of Wicca, and this is the place from which a large number of gods come. Therefore, it tends to be that the gods / goddesses that the individual has chosen to pursue will be seen in all or most of their spells, or on the other hand, gradually large, and the intervals can incorporate the characteristics or traits apply to you. For example, Athena will be used for affection; Brigid will be summoned for recovery.

Wiccans often use images of the wheel of life in their costumes, especially around Saturday time. It will be a piece of the coven's unique tradition of renting the season. It revolves around the primary

God and Goddess, symbolizing the change of seasons. The goddess gives birth to the God who, at that moment, develops during rest and recovery. When it is established, they begin to look at all the starry eyes, and the goddess will become pregnant. As the cycles unfold, God dissolves, and in the long run, his passage is praised in anticipation of his resurrection to Yule!

Similarities in Wiccan Spells / Witchcraft

Both Wiccan and Black magic spells will use all-inclusive components to offer a "charge" to their spells. These components are Air, Fire, Water, Earth and soul, and each has a unique ability to offer. Both Wiccan and witches will go to these ordinary endowments in their spells.

Both traditions will also use common elements of the Earth for their spells. From spell herbs to kindergarten leaves, these venerated blessings are the staples of casting spells for both. This stems from a concern for the universe and the higher forces around us. Nature is both a preeminent ploy and a power, and tends to be direct and won with these fixations using your innate energies.

In any case, to use these fasteners skillfully in the Wiccan and Black magic spells, both types of Wheels train to pinpoint their exceptional abilities to perform their periods. This may require long periods of practical training. The techniques here are bound to vary from one individual to another here, however, as opposed to between Wiccans and witches.

Chapter 18

The Wicca Calendar

The Wiccan calendar follows an eight-year year with eight festivals of the solstice, equinox and the fourth Cross. The year follows a cycle that begins with the birth symbolized by the egg that follows the death symbolized by the fire of the effigies in the neighborhood of the autumn cross. The dates and meanings of these festivals are summarized as follows.

2nd fever-Imbolc

Imbolc is traditionally a time to burn candles. It is also connected with the bride the life force that carries the Earth from winter to spring. Some Wiccan are buying candles right now and burning them to celebrate this festival.

March 21-Spring Equinox

The spring equinox is a time for eggs celebrating New Birth. The consumption of transverse Hot Bread is originally based on the spring equinox with the Cross representing the four quarters of the year. In the Wicca tradition, it makes more sense to eat them at the spring equinox or during the full moon of the egg (the full moon following the spring equinox). The name Easter represents the pagan goddess Eostre, related to eggs, and etymology is related to estrogen related to egg production in humans.

1 May-Beltane

This is Mayday, once for the maypole dance and widely regarded as a fertility festival

June 21-Summer Solstice

The summer solstice is a traditional time for bonfires to celebrate the longest day.

1 August-Lammas

Lammas means bread mass and is the beginning of the detection period, and traditionally the time when the first bread was baked.

September 21-Autumn Equinox

The autumn equinox is the end of the harvest and the time of harvest, feast

October 31-Halloween

Halloween is the time when people traditionally put pumpkin lamps to guide spirits to their homes

December 21-Winter Solstice

The winter solstice is a time for celebrations and the Lord's contribution to the house to prove that the New Year will come.

When repeating Wicca, it is imperative to make the Wicca calendar to repeat the right habits at the right time. These Wicca occasions are typical agnostic occasions when the ceremonies are over. This Wicca calendar specifies what and when there are several occasions. Use this Wicca calendar to find out when to worship and perform costumes. You can also discover explicit ceremonies on explicit occasions.

Big parties or Saturdays:

Halloween, otherwise called Samhain is usually seen on October 31. The most precise time to watch Samhain is the full moon before October 31, however, it is progressively beneficial for people to see October 31 with the current hectic reality. Samhain is the time when all the spirits and minds of this world pass into the other world. That's why we wear sets today.

Woman's Day, or candlestick, congratulated the second of February. This occasion is festive and the expectations of the arrival of life. It is expected to congratulate the arrival of spring, sooner rather than later. The arrival of a new life. It is a stress for spring to come quickly with the goal that plants and foods can be planted and developed again. It is also an opportunity for the Goddess-lady to be invited to return to earth, homes and shrines.

Can Eva, or Beltane congratulate may 1. Beltane is seen to praise the arrival of the glow and the sun. On archaic occasions, it was when the crowd gathered in the mountains to gnaw at the herbs.

Bonfires have often been observed on the landscape, from one exit from the house and the city, and then on the other. Beltane marks half of the Suns' adventure between the spring equinox and the spring solstice. This was hailed as the beginning of the New Year.

On the eve of August, or Lammas congratulates the first of August on the Wicca calendar. This opportunity is monitored and welcomes the main products of the harvest and is mainly on the occasion of the disappearance of the year. Lammas is a feast of generous harvest and food and development.

The small holidays or the Saturday of the Wicca calendar:

The spring ritual congratulates the main spring day. This occasion is actually as the name suggests on the Wicca calendar, the main day of spring. It is seen at the arrival of the spring equinox, and is examined in light of the fact that it indicates the main day that there are more long periods of sunshine than darkness. It is the ritual of birth and the beginning of the harvest of the year. It's one of the good deals, winter and blur.

Summer day is the main day of summer. This opportunity is welcomed with the arrival of mid-year Equinox. This is the longest day of the year and prints the center of the duration of the cycle.

After this day, the days begin to shorten and the nights become longer.

The autumn rite is the first day of autumn and welcomes the arrival of the autumn equinox. This is the time when the evenings start to be longer than the days. It is the last day of the year that the sunny hours are during the evening. This still speaks at the beginning of the cold and dead season. The harvest is over and winter is coming.

This is the perfect opportunity to reflect and reflect on what will happen.

Yule is the main day of winter, or the winter solstice. This is the occasion when Christian Christmas was born. Christmas is the longest night of the year. This is a festival from the beginning of the virus season and the development towards light and heat on the Wicca calendar.

This is an essential plan of the Wicca calendar. In case you need to know more about costumes and rituals performed on these occasions, or little by little what each occasion speaks, you should do more research. The purpose of this section is much more than can be guaranteed.

Chapter 19

A Beginner's Guide to Wiccan Spells and Rituals

The word Wicca handles a kind of black magic. A Wiccan doesn't really mean a person who is a witch, totally in training. So in case you wish to be a Wiccan, you don't need to be a witch repeating this black magic and the same in the other way is invalid. In any case, in case you want to be immediately, that is, a Wiccan repeating black magic, at that moment it is indisputably conceivable. Before you start with this art, you need to know a few things about it, similar to its root and nature.

Wicca is a piece of agnostic religion. It is relatively new, and seems to be continuous progress. His source had something to do with an individual named Gerard Gardner. He was incredibly baffled and felt exasperated by Christianity as a religion and the enchantment engaged in any service. This irritation prompted him to think in an alternative way. This way of thinking offered ascension to Wiccan spells and ceremonies. Many trusted that it appeared during 1951 and some deny this belief by expressing that it began in 1954.

Wicca is a manufacture that makes an individual free and independent. Anyone who discovers Wiccan craftsmanship would be in a situation to include greater imperiousness as part of his character. They develop gradually aware of taking on the results of their own behavior. The brilliant guideline of this know - how expresses "if you do not hurt anyone, do what you want". This implies that this craft should be accustomed to bring a new importance to someone's life, practicing execution in the way it is necessary to injure someone's advantage.

Stealing this craft to achieve the decimation of the lives of others will hurt its creator and not the individual it should. So, this idea unequivocally expresses that this craft was created as another work with a valuable envelope of approach, to illuminate and not bring tragedies and become selfish to realize their own methods. So it develops on a decent and solid way of thinking.

Most Wiccan believes that it is a deplorable demonstration of forcing the way of thinking to other people who do not want to engage with it.

Wiccans accept that in case your goals are not mixed and imperfect, repeating this craft will give you quick results. This is so in light of the fact that your true desires produce a positive vitality that has the ability to make decent changes. So, you can try to gain skills with some other things about less complex spells and ceremonies and find out the reality for yourself.

Wicca is a cult?

Nope. A clique is a strict or otherworldly meeting that follows a pioneer, often follows them blindly and makes things destructive or illicit thoughts. Just like Wicca has no principles, no pioneers. No governing body, no pioneer.

While some Wiccan form gatherings (occasionally called congregations) to reflect, share information, or perform Customs, these are equivalent gatherings with any assigned pioneer (or high priest or Priestess) being an accommodation for rituals and associations beyond an innovator in the traditional sense. Like any meeting, the inner self can be a factor, however, as the Wiccan firmly accept in freedom through and through.".. Do what you want", this is the particular case and many gatherings will quickly self-destruct at random as a party strives to control each of them. Obviously you need to investigate any meeting you plan to join and use your own judgment by staying with them.

Is That Wicca Witchcraft?

While many use the terms interchangeably, Wicca is not witchcraft.

Witchcraft (or" crafting") is a different practice not related to Wicca or any other world. Any trusted person- Christian, Buddhist, Islamic, etc.

- can study or practice witchcraft and this does not make her a Wiccan. Witches can repeat without strict or deep convictions working with pure vitality that they consider only vitality and nothing divine.

Witchcraft uses the field of vitality or God to influence change according to their will. For Wiccans, this again brings harm to no one-Wiccan witches do not work on hexing or what is usually considered a "dark" spell and strive to change themselves more than others.

What do Wiccans do?

As the way you practice is available for every Wiccan to choose for themselves and there are no defined principles as I just said, it tends to be difficult to understand what Wiccan really does. Below are probably the best known practices, but it is not in any way, form or in-depth form.

Most Wiccans contemplate in one form or another. Contemplation is an extraordinary method to calm your mind and expand your faculties to interface or feel God. Some use dynamic thinking practices, such as Yoga (especially Hatha Yoga) instead of sitting down to contemplation. Some find a walk in nature or a dip as the best approach to associating with God.

Most Wiccan respect nature by following the seasons or the cycle of the moon because both affect the degree of vitality they feel.

Although there are no established guidelines or customs, several congregations and creators have attempted to standardize or distribute ceremonies for their own use or guides to New Wiccans. You are in any case free (and generally authorized!) to change these ceremonies distributed or make their own. Connecting with God involves doing it in a way that you think is ideal for you-for some it's clothes, raised special areas, and a complete arrangement of ceremonial Appliances, Latin dialects, or the like. For other people, it just means standing barefoot in the grass and contemplating the full moon.

Many Wiccan are extremely involved in environmental causes and political battles as a technique to influence change.

Would it be a good idea for me to fear Wicca?

As the main standard of Wicca seems to be "one hurt no, do what you want", for the most part, there is nothing to fear from anyone who repeats Wicca. Obviously, there are fans of every otherworldly, so you should rather investigate any person or collection you plan to join.

How to Perform Wiccan Spells and Rituals

Wiccan ritual spells need a good way to study before doing so. Many people want to know how to perform spells and rituals, but do not want to learn the basics. To make Wiccan ritual spells, you need to have a good understanding of their basics. This is what we find in the Book Of Shadows.

But if you are looking for the book, then it makes no sense to look for a single magic book. There is not a single book for Magic; The Book Of Shadows refers to any book or eBook that contains a list of potions, spells, records and references to witches.

But the different parties have always tried to formulate an imaginary book of shadows where people would always want a particular book. This creates misunderstandings, rivalries and not to mention violence. This influenced the ancient art of Wiccan Magic For centuries.

When you want to perform a Wiccan spell or magic, you need to be clear on what you want to achieve and then try to figure out how to achieve it. To find the method, you can collect all the information you want from books, other witches, online and even dreams.

How do I do that ?

But information is never enough. There is always a lot to know, a lot to understand, and you do not know everything. So try to look at new evidence of information and try to understand how this plays a role in the spell you are trying to cast.

For example, let's say you're trying to evoke a deity. The first thing you need to ask is how you can relate to deity in relation to Destiny.

If on the other hand you are looking for matches, you can try to find out how the whole puzzle fits. Correspondence is the art of seeing how one aspect is related to another. This can be illustrated by an example.

There are favorable times and places for performing Wiccan spell rituals. For example, a love spell should be performed on Friday evening. This is because Friday is conventionally considered a good day for casting such spells. So it is better to cast the spell under a wax Moon.

You can summon the goddess Diane, the goddess of the Moon and the hunt. The next step is the important part of writing a spell for the sake of cast iron. In this you can choose to refer to the metaphor of "hunting"with the help of" hunting for love."Then the petals of Red Rose can be burned in the flame of a fire that has been lit with red oak wood. If you do this way, virtually never the object of your batch matches all the other elements that form a perfect set.

But it's not the same for everyone. The items must have a connection with you. So, if the petals of red rose do not seem romantic to you, do not use it. You need to understand what works for you. But this is the basic guideline according to which Wiccan ritual spells must be performed.

Chapter 20

Wicca Information, With Free Spells,

Wicca Symbols and Beliefs for the wicca beginner

This is a straight forward, simple to peruse site that answers every one of your inquiries concerning Wicca, what we accept, why we cast spells and how we raise capacity to accomplish whatever we look for all out outcomes! After almost 40 years of following and rehearsing Wicca in private, and

watching it change and develop, I have chosen to share what I love and know with the world!

The ideal learning instrument for the Wicca Beginner, you can master all that you were constantly inquisitive about in a straightforward simple to understand way! It incorporates a manual for Moon stages and how they relate to spells, and the present moon stage is constantly posted. A not insignificant rundown of Gods and Goddesses is incorporated and a clarification of what everyone speaks to, and why certain Gods and Goddesses are useful and welcome to help with Spells. All fixings expected to create each Spell is given!

It additionally incorporates data about certain things that other Wicca sites don't address, for example, Animism. You will locate an enormous rundown of Herbs alongside a portrayal of their significance when utilized in Spells. Light hues for magic ceremonies are completely clarified. Bit by bit guidelines are incorporated with each Spell and Ritual, and Spells are in every case free!

I have likewise incorporated a guide with the significance of Gems and Crystals and how they are utilized in Witchcraft Rituals. You will discover a rundown of Wicca Terms utilized in this site alongside a clarification of their significance. There are a few Wicca Holidays and Festivals celebrated during the time which is depicted under "Wicca Calendar".

There are numerous misguided judgments flowing about Wicca, which unfortunately is made up by different religions who feel it is significant that we accept the equivalent. There are even books composed just to startle individuals into deduction we are underhanded fiend admirers and ruinous creatures. Nothing could be further from reality! This is a piece of the explanation I have decided to open up and share all I know and love about Wicca!

After you glance through this site you will find that Wicca is excellent, serene and simple to pursue. We never attempt to get you to put stock in anything, considerably less something that you can't see, hear or contact. What's more, not normal for different religions we accept that every kid is brought into the world

Blessed, not conceived in wrongdoing as different religions which expect sanctification to rinse one's spirit.

Chapter 21

Top Tips for Spells

Spell tricks can range from essential pointers for the beginner to pieces of wisdom for the more trained charmer. As much as it may be, we could all do with a little help from time to time and it's far from hard to forget some of the things we learn along the way to becoming an accomplished and vital witch. So I have assembled a tiring of some of what I consider to be the most important tips for spells that I have learned or that have been passed on to me and the expectation that you can find a use in them too! This way, no specific request:

1) One of the best spell tips I can give you in case you are just beginning is when you are looking for other people's spells to perform by going for the spell you are attracted to. This implies that you speak to yourself at the level of clairvoyant Association and will help you be ready to tune in to the correct forces when you perform it. Similarly, do not go for the maximum of out-of-control complaints or more flashy claims. No spell should profess to have a chance to change your life in

the medium term. In any case, this quiet, humble little spell could probably be to implement a little improvement that triggers opportunities that take you where you need to go throughout your daily life.

2) When you write your own, do close to them, you would be careful. Try not to hang up too much to try to duplicate another's style or techniques. Although it can help in the early stages to perceive how others work, you will be constantly gradually powerful in your spell work on the possibility that you can relate to your spell and see your qualities in it.

3) Use large devices. In the end, most witches break on devices made for reason. This can help with the atmosphere and environment of your elevated area or workspace and can also help as they are explicitly structured. So it is not essential and at random you find yourself with a connection to a specific object, at that time you stay with it for the necessary period of time. I had for example a huge bowl that I used for a cauldron

for a very long time! The association is important in contrast to the thing itself.

4) Dedicate any space where you work consistently. Many witches argue that it is constantly essential for you to sanctify the area and the devices you use, but they disagree. In any case, it came to my list of 10 tips for spells because it is an extremely innovative service to instill the belief that everything is good and confidence in the workspace. You will feel that it is gradually Holy and "claimed" by you. The Smearing of lavender and Sage is feasible but simple.

5) Work with excellent ingredients on every occasion. More normal is better you will draw much more power from the resources of the world, for example. In the event that you use new flowers, be sure to cut them yourself on the luck you can.

6) Sixth of my advice for spells is to set. This is a botch for beginners largely and can emerge from being in a race on top to get started. Unfortunately, spells are usually not as beneficial as we would like and you will not have place running. You'll be a progressively

powerful disaster if you find an example of putting yourself in the right attitude. Very well, you can take a relaxing shower surrounded by candles, using reflection or dressing in clothes that you feel give the correct energies. It could also be a combination of each of the 3 however review to find what is ideal for you.

7) In addition to the tips for spells number 6 above, you should at the same time not be in a hurry to see the results. I discovered spells that took a long time to work and ended up being greatly improved for me than I originally imagined! Trust superior wisdom at work and believe that the right moment is at hand.

8) Be reasonable. Great things can be achieved with the correct fate and a lot of hard work, determination and ability. In any case, do not try to duplicate things that you may have found on TV or in the cinema.

9) Work with the seasons or lunar cycles. This is connected with the incorporation of the energies that are around you, known to man. Everything is here to be direct, so why waste! You will understand how to have

the opportunity to perceive the different energies around you as you gradually become adept at drawing them and so you can design your spell in advance.

10) , this might be my last advice for spells, but it's really one of the most important. Remember the evil person of Wiccan Rede. Try not to attempt to do something that could hurt others or attempt to change their freedom through and through. Be aware of your work.

Chapter 22

3 Simple Spells For Beginners

Spells for amateurs is an incredible method to begin on the way of Wicca and black magic. If you truly need to have the option to make ground-breaking spells with next to zero exertion, you need to set aside the effort to think about and learn and apply that data. The more in order you get with the universe and your general surroundings, the more dominant your spells will be. A fledgling enchanting won't get indistinguishable outcomes from somebody who has been rehearsing for a long time. Here are a few spells for tenderfoots to begin with and to begin building up your characteristic power.

First Of 3 Spells:

To Gain Money

Get a cauldron. A huge bowl will work fine, particularly if you can locate a metal bowl. A cauldron is utilized distinctly for otherworldly purposes, so it is more dominant, be that as it may, it isn't vital. Fill the cauldron or bowl half full of water and position it outside where you expect to do the spell so the light from the moon sparkles into the water. Clear your hands over the water as though assembling the moons silver.

While doing this say:

"Flawless woman of the moon, present to me your riches right soon. Fill my hands with silver and gold.

All you give, my tote can hold."

Second Spells:

To Gain Love

Start by getting some virgin olive oil and spot it in a dull, glass compartment. Fill it with flower petals and let it sit for at any rate seven days. Strain the oil from the petals and spot back in the glass holder.

This can be utilized as an oil for any adoration enchantment you wish to do. You can likewise buy an affection oil at your neighborhood agnostic shop. Get two red decreased candles and spot them on a table one next to the other.

Between the two candles, place an incense burner. Coat the candles in the adoration oil. At the point when you are prepared to start, light the candles.

Spot a bit of charcoal in the incense burner and over it sprinkle dried flower petals. Present the accompanying chant:

"Light of intensity, flame of might, Make my wants here on this night. Bring me love, present to me a date, Bring to me my extraordinary mate.

Power, stream from this current flame's fire.

 Bring to me my deepest longing.

My words have quality, the triumph's won. So state I, this spell is finished."

Third Spells:

To Lose Weight

Get yourself a gold emblem and have the resemblance of a fish engraved on it. You can discover this at practically any great adornments store. A little, plane emblem will do fine. If not, the intensity of the web is splendid.

Serenade the accompanying over the engraved emblem:

"Brilliant fish, I wear you,

In the conviction that you will make me slender and excellent. Check my eating, and let me eat fish and great nourishment. That will make me flimsy."

Presently wear the emblem and stop eating so much junk food. The pounds will liquefy away with no battle and remaining to your eating routine will be incredibly simple.

Here are only a couple of spells for tenderfoots that you can utilize at the present time. Recall however, to get the best outcomes with spells, you should utilize them, you should learn, you should rehearse and develop.

The more astute you are, the more dominant you are. The more dominant you are, the more dominant your spells become. A decent educator, program, or a truck heap of books will assist you with learning and develop.

Chapter 23

Wicca Symbols Explained

There is a wide range of images used in Wicca that a real specialist must think about. These Wicca images speak of various types of vitality and parts of the deep world. The most essential to understand and build an association regarding Wicca images are the fundamental components. These are the establishment of all that is physical that you can contact. So, we should start our investigation.

Earth is the first of the components we need to discuss when it comes to Wicca images. The image of the Earth is a tortuous triangle with a regular line running through it. The Earth is the creation of everything. It speaks of solidity, vision, strength, wealth, material wealth and development.

The Earth is also spoken on a compass like the North. He talks to the Heavenly assistant Raphael and is managed by the planet Mercury. Build an understanding of this component because it creates everything. This is the physical world, and this is where our food comes from. In addition, the way it gives us a place to live. That's why it's been alluded to Mother Earth for so long. It nourishes us, dresses US, supports us and gives us a home and a home.

Water is the next component that we need to discuss. The water is still strong, but it begins to push towards the area of components that cannot be contacted. All components can be tested, but you can not get a handful of water a handful of land. The image of water is a tortuous triangle. Water speaks of intuition, change, flow, instinct, inner information, compassion and love.

The West is the Cardinal landing spoken with water. Gabrielle is the Messenger bound to the holy water and the planet bound to the water is the moon. Water is the following of Wicca pictures to understand. It is the embodiment of human life. Without water, we'd all bite the dust. This is the most fundamental component of resistance.

Fire is the third of the Wicca images and is spoken from a triangle upwards. Fire speaks to these energies of extension, direct responsibility, courage, cleanliness, inventiveness, the Higher Self and the will to leave.

The West is the cardinal port of fire and Michael is the Blessed Messenger spoken by fire. The sun is the planet tied to fire. Fire is the next component as it can also be seen but never contacted or has a handle on. As we climb the component diagram, we begin to move into territories that can be lived, but are not contacted or tasted like rocks and soil. Fire is essential for heat and cooking.

Air is the Fourth of Wicca images to build an understanding and its image is an ascending triangle with a uniform line through the center. The air is spoken south on the compass and incorporates parts of correspondence, immediacy, concentration, sympathy, sending warrior, giving, concern and sympathy.

The planet Venus is tied to the aerial component, and Ariel is the Heavenly assistant. Air is that part of breathing, opportunity and development that is important for the realization and joy of every living animal.

The soul is the fifth and last of the Wicca images we will talk about here. The core is located on the Compass directly in the center of the different components. It is harmony between all and complements the ability to move from one, then to the side effortlessly. It talks about understanding the different components. The soul is everything and everything is for the soul.

The soul is spoken by the planet Saturn. Holy Messenger Cassel.

Build an understanding of these Wicca images and use them consistently. As you develop your feedback and learn how to be a witch and a Wiccan expert, your understanding of these components will be meaningful to your development.

Chapter 24

Wicca Symbols and What They Can Mean to You

Wicca images have been with us for a considerable length of time yet are still as pertinent to cutting edge Pagans and Wiccans as they ever were. Despite the fact that there is some variety in the images from gathering to gathering, they are all the more frequently reliable in the conditions that they speak to than not. This is an article on the absolute generally famous and intense images, which I have picked in light of the fact that to me, they most unequivocally encapsulate Wicca and a big motivator for it.

One of the most immediately conspicuous of Wicca images is that of the pentacle - otherwise called the Witch's Foot. It is a 5 point star around and each point speaks to (going clockwise and beginning at the top):

The Spirit Earth

Air Fire Water

The hover around them brings together and ties them all. This Wicca image is critical and ground-breaking as it speaks to you and your place inside the world and its components - you are the soul.

This is simply the image that Wiccans wear to recognize themselves as well as other people with, making it the most recognizable characteristic of the Wiccan religion. It is worn proudly, and to stamp the wearer's devotion to, and regard for nature.

Be that as it may, wearing this Wicca image isn't without potential issues. There has for quite some time been an incredible misunderstanding that Wicca is some way or another associated with dim powers, even Satanism. Luckily, this couldn't possibly be more off-base. Indeed, the wearer is expressing that they are on a Magical way, however one which will remove them from insidious, not towards it. It implies their longing to love and respect natures in the entirety of its structures, and with deference for its extraordinary power. It is an individual vow to provide for nature and not to take from it pointlessly.

Fundamentally the same as the pentacle, is the Wicca image of the pentagram - the 5 pointed star of the pentacle however which stands alone. This dynamic image speaks to the flawlessness found in nature and might be more well-known to you than you might suspect

- consider Leonardo Da Vinci's Vitruvian Man! Pythagoreans likewise saw it as a scientific flawlessness. As much misjudged as the pentacle, it has additionally been viewed as associated with dull powers, especially when modified.

In any case, there are signs that things are changing and Wicca is beginning to shake off these old style sees. In April of 2007 in America, it was decided that the pentacle would be perceived and gave in military graveyards and for gravestones, where beforehand this had been denied.

Anyway, what do the individual Wicca images that make up the pentagram speak to in themselves?

Earth is some of the time shaped as a Wicca image by utilizing the quartered circle, the ideal cross inside the circle or then again as a reversed triangle with a flat line most of the way up. The image of earth is a female vitality - earth and Mother Nature are regularly one and the equivalent. It is the very establishment of our reality.

The Wicca image of air is nearly equivalent to the triangle image for earth however the triangle is upstanding. This component is surrounding us, basic forever itself yet additionally imperceptible so a component that we can without much of a stretch underestimate. This image urges us to respect and regard it. On Wiccan special stepped areas, incense is frequently utilized on the east to speak to air.

Water and fire additionally utilize the triangle yet without the lines through them. Fire is upstanding and water is transformed.

The power and damaging intensity of fire can't be mixed up. It is wondrous to observe when contained, yet there is an ever present sense that it could take control from your hands whenever. This Wicca image goes about as both an update and an admonition to pay attention to the extraordinary power that nature can be.

Water is the supplier of life just as profound and secretive. Numerous individuals find that they have an extraordinary partiality with water and the ocean, more so than different components as it appears to exemplify such a large number of human feelings and qualities. It is hard not to stand and watch the sea without feeling at one with it.

These center Wicca images are just a couple of the hundreds that you can concentrate to assist your understanding of both Wiccan and the planet that we occupy, ingraining a regard that will make you feel progressively complete.

Chapter 25

Astrology in Wicca

Most witches have some confidence in crystal gazing. We acknowledge that the situation of the planets impacts our introduction to the world which figures out what our identity is and our future lives. It must be recalled that they are just impacts, different factors, for example, through and through freedom, hereditary qualities and chance are additionally influencing everything.

To get soothsaying, your introduction to the world diagram is a decent spot to begin. Your natal outline is individual explicit dependent on date, time and your place of birth. A celestial prophet would have the option to translate numerous things from this to precisely reveal to you things about yourself and your life.

Having your introduction to the world graph done expertly can be over the top expensive, in any case, there are books which can assist you with doing your own. The outcomes can be extremely uncovering. Natal graphs can likewise be gotten to on the web.

Your introduction to the world outline could assist you with acknowledging whether you have lived previously. On the off chance that your outline has an absence of Karma, it could demonstrate that

your are another spirit. Bunches of Karma is a certain fire pointer of an Old Soul.

As some time in the past as 30000 BC early people have been diagramming the stars. Chaldeans from Assyria initially recorded that stars ran in a specific request, while planets moved around. As planets went before the fixed stars, groups of stars, the occasions of people appeared to connect with the planet in question. At the point when Mars was unmistakable, people appeared to be prepared for the fight to come, while when Venus was obvious, it appeared to advance harmony. Mars known as the God of War and Venus, The Goddess of Love. Crystal gazing as we probably am aware it today started around 700 BC.

Over longer timeframes, more connections between the situating of the stars and planets were watched and confirmed. It turned out to be certain that this foreknowledge could be utilized as a preferred position for rulers, nations and realms. Soothsaying is digging in for the long haul.

The Sun Signs rule everything. It is simply the part that you show to other people and is difficult to stow away. Your sun sign is the one you read in the papers about your horoscope. You can share a few attributes of the sign beside yours in the event that you are on the cusp, ie. A couple of days from the sign nearest to you.

The sky is separated into 12, every segment being known as a house. Houses spread every zone of human advancement.

Contingent upon which planet or star grouping lies in which house, we can accumulate pieces of information to the territory that will be impacted. The planet in the house shows how something will show while the heavenly body shows the way of its indication.

House Representations

First House - Birth

Fundamental character, physical wellbeing, physical appearance and the manner in which you uncover yourself to other people

Second House - Possessions

Riches, material belongings, individual things and emotions

Third House - Mind

Correspondence, how you convey what needs be and how you consider the world

Fourth House - Home

Where you live, your foundations, lineage, guardians and family

Fifth House - Creativity

Joy, relaxation and mingling

Sixth House - Work

Work, business, vocation openings and working connections

Seventh House - Heart

Connections and relationships, marriage and long haul accomplices

Eighth House - Sharing

Demeanors toward sex, cash and thoughts. Uncovers liberality or absence of

Ninth House - Intellect

Learning, training, childhood and furthermore study as a grown-up

Tenth House - Personal Ambitions

Desires, dreams, objectives, longings and drives

Eleventh House - Friendship

Engaging companions and social associates yet in addition the manner in which you enjoy individual delights

12 House - Escapism

Withdrawal, depression, passing and the oblivious. It speaks to your feelings of trepidation.

Chapter 26

Witch Spells How They Work & How to Write Your Own

A witch spell is a vitality that is made and diverted by you, either all alone or in a gathering, so as to impact a change and get something going. That 'something' could be exceptionally close to home (to bring love into your life) or increasingly wide (to help with the season's reap - not all that regular these days!). It tends to be communicated in words and customs or in calm examination.

You fabricate a witch spell's capacity from rationally anticipating your confidence, emotions and perceptions however you can likewise strengthen this power with the utilization of materials, for example, candles, incense, precious stones and herbs.

Are Wiccan Spells Different to Witch's Spells?

Not really as both revolve around fundamentally the same as strategies. This is on the grounds that truly,

Wicca and witch share similar roots, and Wicca took on its name so as to disassociate itself from the disgrace and mistreatment that had become connected the term 'witch'. In any case, while Wiccan spells can be close to home you will likewise have the advantage of your coven's understanding and aggregate spells to work with. Witch spells are all the more frequently of the individual kind as it were.

It is a center piece of the Wiccan religion to function as though at one with all the universe, the aggregate power of its components being more dominant than any of only them, and this is the reason the pentagram is their strict image. Numerous singular witches profit by this rule too as it advances regard for our general surroundings so regardless of whether you don't contemplate some other piece of Wicca, turn this upward!

Terrible Spells and Good Spells

It is an acknowledged all inclusive law that when you play out a spell you will get back the vitality that you channel into it. Some even accept that this will return three-crease. Thus, an expression of caution about throwing negative spells or hexes on others.

This will return to you as the originator of the vitality so you might need to hold up under at the top of the priority list the well-known adage, 'be cautious what you wish for'!

Concentrate your energies on positive occasions and attempt to go for spells that will contribute, not exclusively to your life, however to others' lives and the world in general.

Step by step instructions to Perform A Witch Spell

Ensure that you have arranged! It is anything but a smart thought to simply attempt to 'make things up along the way'. You'll think that its harder than you envision. Accumulate your composed spell, materials and take yourself to a calm space where you won't be upset.

In the event that you need to perform spells all the time, at that point you might need to set up a Wiccan special stepped area for this reason. Once more, what you keep on your special stepped area is a totally close to home issue yet consistently keep your book of shadows (your diary for keeping takes note of), your elements for your present spell and any apparatuses you'll have to hand so as not to upset the stream.

Your Own Spell Versus Someone Else's

You may imagine that it is simpler to perform spells that somebody increasingly experienced has composed, or ones that were made numerous years back. They can be viable absolutely, and furthermore supportive in the good 'ol days when you need certainty. Nonetheless, your own spells will be even more dominant in light of the fact that your energies will be direct so take a stab at composing your own as quickly as time permits.

Traditionally, witch spells have come in rhyme yet you don't have to stress over this on the off chance that it implies that you'll battle. In any case, rhymes can construct mood and a feeling of fun so on the off chance that it comes to you in this structure, accept the way things are.

Composing Your Own Witch Spells

Composing witch spells is an ability that you will expand upon after some time so start basic. The impacts of passing up a great opportunity something basic can be more awful than not having endeavored the spell at all so be mindful so as not to overstretch yourself. Here are some fundamental tips on what to remember for your own witch spells:

Try not to be too explicit about what you need. In the event that you need another vehicle, attempt not concentrate a lot on a particular model as the Gods and Goddesses may know about something more qualified to your needs thus you might be constraining what you will get.

Try not to be excessively unclear! It seems like an inconsistency to the above point at the same time, adhering to the case of the vehicle, when you request divine assistance incorporate your purposes behind needing it, eg. So as to get the opportunity to work, to see family. This legitimizes your reasons and furthermore can forestall you being given the vehicle and afterward finding that it will just get you to the highest point of the street!

Attempt to ensure what you request is for more prominent's benefit and not only for altogether childish reasons. Once more, recollect that you are diverting vitality.

Utilize visual prompts on the off chance that you discover it encourages you. Get a photograph of what you need and spot it before you as you play out your spell.

Request help from the Gods and Goddesses to fill in anything you may have forgotten about. In the event that you've placed enough idea and exertion into your spell, divine help ought to be inevitable.

Love spells

It was once emphatically accepted that witches could have intercourse mixtures sufficiently amazing to change an individual's unrestrained choice - one of the most celebrated cases being Henry VIII who was supposedly caught by Anne Boleyn along these lines! In any case, it isn't as straightforward as that and in the event that somebody isn't slanted to be in love with you, at that point an elixir or spell won't change that reality.

Notwithstanding, there are things you can do to give the normal course of love a little help!

There are sure fixings that are useful for love spells so get hold of, and try different things with:

Rose quartz Amethyst Pink candles

Pink or red harmony

The main blossoms of spring, for example, daffodils Violets are another great 'love' blossom

The herb basil Blue poppy seeds

Catmint (catnip) Spell Candles

A great method to begin with a straightforward but then exceptionally

compelling witch spell is to utilize a light. Certain hues carry with them certain energies and by joining this vitality with one of the center components, to be specific fire, you increment its strength. So as to make the spell successful you should set aside an opportunity to sit before the flame and focus on what you need to occur. It is smarter to attempt it in one go yet it is additionally fine to consume the light more than 3 nights.

You should envision the future and envision yourself as in love, obtaining a sizable sum of wealth or whatever it is you want.

In the case of utilizing blessing oils, go from base to top for expanding spells and the other path round for banishing or decreasing.

Keep in mind, the guidelines of the universe are frequently exceptionally basic and fuse great old sound judgment. Try not to victory your light on the off chance that it is absurd to expect to torch it the whole distance, utilize a snuffer as you would prefer not to overwhelm the entirety of the charged vitality you've figured out how to develop.

Chapter 27

Misconceptions About Wicca

I am here not to guard Wicca as a religion, however I am to express a few certainties about their convictions. Witches have consistently been related with old women with pointy nose, long nails, and broomsticks. This isn't valid for course.

As everyone should realize witches is one of the terms related with individuals rehearsing Wicca. There is additionally nothing of the sort as malevolent or great witch in Wicca. Wiccans don't have a severe idea of what is detestable and what is great. It is somewhere down in oneself that, that judgment will be passed. Wiccans accept that the main time an individual submits an improper demonstration is on the off chance that he figures it may have insulted his convictions as an individual, or might have annoyed others. Being liable for one's activities is a significant part in the Wiccan conviction framework. It shows them on the proper behavior on their decisions, and recognizes what is generally insightful to do. Another misguided judgment about Wicca is that they're Satanists. This is something that they have cleared from the time that they have been built up as a religion.

One of the most significant Wiccan images is the pentagram. It speaks to the 5 components that are exceptionally revered in Wicca; earth, air, fire, water, and soul. Be that as it may, the Wiccan pentagram intently takes after the rearranged pentagram utilized by the Church of Satan. This is what's befuddling the general population about Wicca. Judgment has just been made to the adherents, and it made a social shame, that as of recently is broadly accepted by a greater part of individuals.

Another misguided judgment is that Wiccans practice Black Magic. The idea of good and awful is obscure to numerous witches. Wicca has consistently advanced the utilization of magic to help others when they need profound direction. Besides, dark magic signifies that there is malicious in the hearts of Wiccans. This is only unfounded incriminations to Wiccans. There has been no strong evidence of dark magic spells being caused on others. Wiccans have consistently sustained their otherworldliness by utilizing magic as a method for contemplation and reflection.

One final misguided judgment that I need to call attention to is this. Wiccans are not moronic, uneducated individuals. A few Wiccans that I for one know are those with high mind. Wiccans, the two traditionalists and solitaries have been found in the field of science innovation, and business. Wiccans are not about Wiccan spells and cauldrons. They are those individuals who know a great deal of things about the world. On the off chance that Wiccans were uneducated rovers, which tabloids guarantee they will be, they would have shaped silly developments or exercises in the avenues.

Rather they keep quiet. It is just the individuals who comprehend the world, and have inward harmony who can quiet out every one of the partialities that the current society still has about Wicca.

www.ingramcontent.com/pod-product-compliance
Lightning Source LLC
Chambersburg PA
CBHW071631080526
44588CB00010B/1357